My
COLORING BIBLE

Alphabetically

Oliver Martin Okoth

authorHOUSE®

AuthorHouse™ UK
1663 Liberty Drive
Bloomington, IN 47403   USA
www.authorhouse.co.uk
Phone: 0800.197.4150

Published by AuthorHouse   08/03/2016

ISBN: 978-1-5246-6167-0 (sc)
ISBN: 978-1-5246-6168-7 (e)

Print information available on the last page.

*Any people depicted in stock imagery provided by Thinkstock are models,
and such images are being used for illustrative purposes only.
Certain stock imagery © Thinkstock.*

This book is printed on acid-free paper.

Scripture quotations marked KJV are from the Holy Bible, King James Version (Authorized Version). First published
in 1611. Quoted from the KJV Classic Reference Bible, Copyright © 1983 by The Zondervan Corporation.

A a. Abraham.

Genesis 22:1-19. God gave Abraham a son called Isaac, whom he asked to sacrifice to test his faith. Abraham obeyed God but when he was about to sacrifice Isaac God told him to spare the child. In his place God provided a ram. It is said 'In the Lord's Mountain he will provide'.

B b. Babel.

Genesis 11:1-9. The people of earth spoke one language at one time; they tried to build a tower to reach the heavens because of their unity. God mixed up the languages and they stopped building the tower of Babel. God scattered man all over the world by taking away their unifying language.

C c. Cain.

Genesis 4:1-16. Cain the son of Adam and Eve murdered his brother Abel because of jealousy. God accepted Abel's sacrifices because he offered his best and rejected Cain's which was not his best. This made him jealous of his brother.

D d. Daniel.

Daniel 6:1-24. Daniel was thrown into a lions' den because of his faith in God. God saved Daniel from the lions.

E e. Elijah.

Kings 18:1-40. Elijah was a prophet of God who called fire from heave to burn his offerings. The prophets of baal could not do the same because baal was not a true god.

F f. Father.

Luke 15:11-32. God is our father and He always loves us no matter what we do. The prodigal son went back to his father after misusing his inheritance and his father forgave him. God is also happy and willing to forgive us when we stop sinning and return to Him.

G g. Goliath.

1 Samuel 17:1-54. Goliath was a giant Philistine soldier whom everyone was scared of. David defeated Goliath with only a sling and a stone because of his faith in God.

H h. Healing.

Luke 7:1-10, Mathew 8:5-13. Jesus is our healer. He healed many people like the centurion servant because of their great faith. We should pray to Him every time we are sick or troubled and believe in His healing.

11. Israel.

Genesis 32:22-32. Jacob fought with God and prevailed and his name was changed from Jacob to Israel.

J j. Jesus.

John 3:16 God loved the world and gave his only son Jesus as a sacrifice for our sins. We should believe in Him so that we don't perish and to have everlasting life.

K k. Kings.

Daniel 3: 1-30.The bible has many stories on different kings. King Nebuchadnezzar threw three friends in a furnace for not worshiping his golden statue. The three friends believed in Jesus who is the King of kings and did not burn.

L l. Lot.

Genesis 19:1-29. Lot left Sodom with his daughters and wife because it was a sinful city which God destroyed with fire. God told them to run and not look back but Lot's wife disobeyed. She looked back and turned into a pillar of salt.

M m. Moses.

The book of Exodus. Moses was a prophet of God who led the Israelites from Egypt and parted the Red sea on their way to the Promised Land.

N n. Noah.

Genesis 6-9. God told Noah to build an Ark in preparation of the floods. The animals, which entered in pairs of male and female, and Noah's family were the only ones saved from the floods.

O o. Obedience.

Samuel 15:10-34. Saul, Israel's first king, was not obedient to God and an evil spirit filled his life with terror. David played the harp to keep him calm.

P p. Paul.

Acts 9:1-19. Paul was one of the greatest followers of Christ. Before he was converted on his way to Damascus, he was called Saul who was one of the Christians worst persecutors.

Q q. Queen.

1st Kings 10:1-13. The queen of Sheba heard of King Solomon's wisdom and travelled to Jerusalem to see the wisest man on earth.

R r. Ruth.

Ruth, a book in the Old Testament, is a story about a loyal woman who did not abandon her mother in law after her husband's death. She married a second husband Boaz and was the great grandmother of King David. Loyalty has its rewards.

S s. Samson.

Judges 13-16. Samson was one of the judges. He defended the Israelites against the Philistines. He was the strongest man ever to live in the earth.

T t. Ten Commandments.

Exodus 20:1-17.God gave Moses the Ten Commandments. They are a set of Ten laws that govern how we should live daily.

U u. Universe.

Genesis 1-2. God created the universe in six days and rested on the seventh, which is the Sabbath day.

V v. Vineyard.

Mathew 21: 33-46. Mark 12: 1-12. Luke 20:9-18. Jesus always taught in parables- a story to bring out an important moral truth. One such parable is the parable of the tenants in the vineyard.

W w. Whale.

The book of Jonah in the Old Testament tells of the prophet Jonah who refused to go to Nineveh as God had instructed him. When trying to run from God by sea, a storm came. He was tossed out of his ship and a big fish swallowed him. He spent three days and nights in the fish and finally went to Nineveh. We cannot run from Gods plans.

X x. Xerxes.

Book of Esther old testament tells of a king called Xerxes who married Esther and he was able to protect the Israelites through her and his servant Mordecai.

Y y. Yeast.

Mathew 13:33 Luke 13:20 Jesus compared the kingdom of heaven to a woman who mixed forty liters of flour with yeast until the whole batch of dough rose.

Z z. Zacchaeus Luke 19:1-9.

Zacchaeus was a short man who climbed a Sycamore tree to see Jesus in a crowd of people. Jesus saw him and told him to get down then went to eat at his house. Zacchaeus was so pleased that he gave half of his wealth to the poor.

Printed in the United States
By Bookmasters